DISCARDED

Canadian Families
CANADIANS AT HOME

TRUE NORTH

BY MARTY GITLIN

True North is published by Beech Street Books
27 Stewart Rd. Collingwood, ON Canada L9Y 4M7

www.beechstreetbooks.ca

Produced by Red Line Editorial

Photographs ©: monkeybusinessimages/iStockphoto, cover, 1; India Picture/Shutterstock Images, 4–5; Red Line Editorial, 6–7; Sergei Bachlakov/Shutterstock Images, 8–9; mikecphoto/Shutterstock Images, 10–11; Buchanan-Hermit, 12–13; Joshua Resnick/Shutterstock Images, 14–15; Nejron Photo/Shutterstock Images, 16; stlee000/iStockphoto, 18–19; Jeff Whyte/Shutterstock Images, 20–21

Editor: Heather C. Hudak
Designer: Laura Polzin

Library and Archives Canada Cataloguing in Publication

Gitlin, Marty, author
    Canadians at home / by Marty Gitlin.

 (Canadian families)
Includes bibliographical references and index.
Issued in print and electronic formats.
ISBN 978-1-77308-009-3 (hardback).--ISBN 978-1-77308-037-6
(paperback).--ISBN 978-1-77308-065-9 (pdf).--ISBN 978-1-77308-093-2
(html)

    1. Dwellings--Canada--Juvenile literature. I. Title.

GT228.G58 2016   j392.3'60971   C2016-903172-1
                                              C2016-903173-X

Printed in the United States of America
Mankato, MN
August 2016

TABLE OF CONTENTS

Chapter One

WHAT IS A FAMILY?

There is no average Canadian family. A family can be large or small. It can have no children or many children. No two families are exactly alike. But they often have a lot in common, too.

Most Canadians live at home with their families. Their homes come in all shapes and sizes. Like the families that live in them, they too can be large or small. Today, there are many one-parent homes. And people are having fewer kids. The average Canadian family has three people. Parents can be two women, two men, or a man and a woman. Parents could be married or not married.

Canadian families can be big or small.

Chapter Two

CANADIAN COMMUNITIES

Canada welcomes people from all over the world. More than one in five Canadians are born in other countries.

People move to Canada for many reasons. Canada has a better quality of life than many countries. And it has very good schools. Canada has been named one of the best places in the world to live. People know they will be welcomed in Canada.

Most Canadian **immigrants** live in Toronto, Montreal, or Vancouver. These cities have the biggest **populations** in Canada. Still, only one third of all Canadians call these

This map shows the 10 most common countries of origin for people who became permanent residents of Canada in 2014.

CANADA'S NEW RESIDENTS

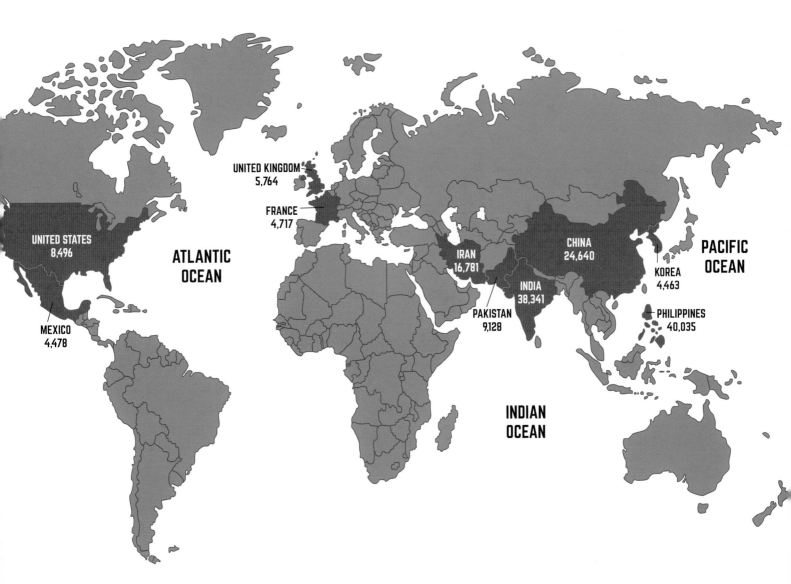

UNITED KINGDOM
5,764

FRANCE
4,717

UNITED STATES
8,496

ATLANTIC OCEAN

MEXICO
4,478

IRAN
16,781

PAKISTAN
9,128

INDIA
38,341

CHINA
24,640

KOREA
4,463

PACIFIC OCEAN

PHILIPPINES
40,035

INDIAN OCEAN

cities home. You can find people from all around the world in many cities, towns, and communities across Canada.

More than half of all Canadian immigrants were born in Asian nations. These include China, Vietnam, Japan, South Korea, Pakistan, India, and the Philippines. Many people born in Africa have made Canada their home as well. More than half of all Africans in Canada live in Ontario.

Aboriginal Peoples live in all parts of the country. The number of First Nations people has risen to nearly one million. Many live in small communities called reserves. There are more than 630 First Nations communities in Canada.

FAST FACT

Immigrants bring the language of their homeland with them. Many Canadians speak more than one language. Almost three in four people who live in Quebec speak only French at home. About the same number of people in the rest of Canada speak only English at home.

Dancers take part in the Squamish Nation Powwow in West Vancouver each year.

 DIFFERENT CULTURES

Many Canadians decorate their homes to show pride in their **heritage**. But the style of their homes reflects the part of the country they live in. Most people in Canada live in houses. Some live in apartments or **condominiums**. There are a wide variety of homes in Canada.

Nova Scotia and Newfoundland and Labrador were among the first parts of Canada settled by Europeans. Many of the houses in these provinces are more than 100 years old. Quite a few settlers in this area were from France. French homes at that time were often made from wood and stone. The settlers

Peggy's Cove in Nova Scotia

used the same materials. They needed to clear the land of trees. They used the logs to build their homes.

Many homes in Calgary are quite modern and large. They reflect the wealth of the local oil industry. In Victoria, British Columbia, the weather is warmer. There are many cottages. Houses in huge **suburban** areas outside Toronto and Montreal are often surrounded by green spaces. These may include gardens or parks. They come to life in spring and summer.

A longhouse at the University of British Columbia

Chapter Four

WHAT'S FOR DINNER?

You could travel to a different Canadian home each day and never eat the same meal twice. Canadian **cultures** are diverse. And so are the foods Canadians eat at home. People living in fishing villages, small towns, and large cities all eat different types of foods.

Some people eat foods from their native lands. People from Asia often use fresh fish in their meals. Many of them live in British Columbia. Fish is common in British Columbia because the province borders the Pacific Ocean.

Canadians from India often eat curry dishes.

Chokecherries are grown in Manitoba and Saskatchewan. Some people use these berries in homemade jams and jellies. They may even use them to make wine.

Some families sell homemade jams and jellies at farmers' markets.

Quebec has many types of French-Canadian foods. One is poutine. It is made of French fries with cheese **curds** and gravy. Another is a meat pie called tourtière. Jewish people brought smoked meat and bagels to Montreal. Many Eastern Europeans eat potato dumplings, such as **pierogies**.

Some parts of Canada are known for producing certain foods. Much of Canada's beef comes from Alberta. Many families have barbecues in the summer. They invite people to their homes for a steak dinner.

Provinces near the Atlantic Ocean are famous for seafood. New Brunswick and Nova Scotia are known for their lobster and cod. People often throw house parties where these are the main dishes.

Chapter Five

HOME SWEET HOME

Canadians often decorate their homes based on their culture. Many Canadians use decorations to show religious pride during the holidays. Ukrainian Catholics often display painted eggs at Easter. Millions of Canadians decorate Christmas trees during the holiday season in December. Jewish people might display a **menorah** during **Hanukkah**.

People from Scotland sometimes have **tartans** in their homes. Tartans are made from a woollen cloth. They have a plaid pattern and come in many colours. People may display tartan blankets or **tapestries**.

Many people from Thailand, Cambodia, Laos, and Burma have spirit houses at their homes.

FAST FACT

Many Asian people have **shrines** in their homes. These objects are used to honour their religion. Some Asian families decorate their homes using feng shui. This concept promotes peace of mind. They may place chairs close together and facing each other, for example. Bedrooms are free of work objects, such as computers. Plants are also popular in bedrooms.

FAST FACT

A well-known Canadian product is the Hudson's Bay point blanket. It has red, yellow, blue, and green stripes. More than 300 years ago, traders built posts in Canada. They made blankets to sell to Aboriginal Peoples and French Canadians.

Canadian homes often have décor from the part of the country they are in. Homes in fishing villages near the coasts may have ocean-themed decorations. Wood furniture and art made by Aboriginal Peoples are common in western and northwestern Canada.

There are many different kinds of homes and families in Canada. Some are big. Others are small. Some live in cities. Others live in small towns. No matter their size or where they live, culture is an important part of family life in Canada.

INQUIRY QUESTIONS

What items do you have in your home that show your family's heritage? How does where you live change the type of home you live in?

The Hudson's Bay blanket is still common across Canada.

GLOSSARY

CONDOMINIUMS
buildings with many individual apartments or houses that are owned by the people living in them

CULTURES
ways of life based on region, country, or ethnic background

CURDS
a thick, white substance that forms when milk sours

HANUKKAH
a Jewish holiday that is celebrated over eight days and nights in late November or December

HERITAGE
something that belongs to someone by birth

IMMIGRANTS
people who move from one country to another

MENORAH
a candleholder with seven or nine branches used during Hanukkah

PIEROGIES
pockets of dough with a filling inside

POPULATIONS
all of the people living in a certain place

SHRINES
hallowed places or objects

SUBURBAN
from a heavily populated area outside a large city

TAPESTRIES
heavy fabrics used in wall hangings and furniture

TARTANS
woollen cloths with a special pattern

22

TO LEARN MORE

BOOKS

Bowers, Vivien. *Wow Canada! Exploring This Land from Coast to Coast*. Toronto: Owlkids Books, 2010.

Greenwood, Barbara. *The Kids Book of Canada*. Toronto: Kids Can Press, 2007.

Hacker, Carlotta: *The Kids Book of Canadian History*. Toronto: Kids Can Press, 2009.

WEBSITES

Canada: TIME for Kids
www.timeforkids.com/destination/canada

Canadian Geographic Kids
www.canadiangeographic.ca/kids

KidZone: Canada's Territories and Provinces
www.kidzone.ws/geography/provinces.htm

National Geographic Kids: Canada Country Profile kids
www.kids.nationalgeographic.com/explore/countries/canada

INDEX

ABOUT THE AUTHOR

Marty Gitlin is an educational book author. He has had more than 100 nonfiction books published. He won more than 45 awards as a newspaper writer.

24

DISCARDED